Pauline H

Talk To The Paw

Whisky & Beards Publishing

WhiskyandBeards.co.uk

Copyright © 2021 by Pauline Holmes

All rights reserved. No part of this publication may be reproduced, distributed, or transmitted in any form or by any means, including photocopying, recording, or other electronic or mechanical methods, without prior written permission of the publisher, except in the case of brief quotations embodied in critical reviews and certain other non-commercial uses permitted by copyright law.

For permission requests, contact the publisher or author.

First published 2021

Copyedited by Jessica Taggart Rose

Edited by Whisky & Beards Publishing

Cover illustration by Cathy Chilly

Author photo by Benjamin Bowles (www.benjaminfilmphotography.co.uk)

Printed in the U.K. by Cloc Book Print

This book has been produced using public funding by Arts Council England

ISBN: 978-1-9160962-5-7

Dear Reader

This is unashamedly a poetry book for dog lovers. Real dog lovers. Those of us who involve our dogs in every aspect of our lives. It's for people who shrug off pawprints on their duvets and greet people at the door with a smile and the phrase *please excuse the mess*.

To us, the dogs that share our homes are more than companions. They're our teachers, guides and friends. We celebrate their quirks and mourn their passing. Not everybody 'gets' us, some think we're odd, eccentric even. I say, hurray for eccentricity.

The dog lovers in my life are among the kindest, most empathic people I know. I love bumping into you at the park, and chatting while our dogs play at our feet.

I'd like to say thank you to my friend Cathy Chilly for doing the artwork on the front cover. You have a great talent. Huge hugs to you and the wonderful Bella.

My best mate Sue also needs a mention. We have such fun together playing with our dogs. Back in the days when Lizzie was hanging off my trouser leg as a puppy, it was Sue who helped me change her from gremlin to gorgeous.

These poems are about real people, real dogs and real events, although, some dogs' names have been changed to spare their blushes.

Thank you for picking up this book. I hope you enjoy it. One note of caution: reading these poems may make you want to rush off and snog your dog.

    Well, that's what I hope, anyway.

Pauline Holmes

PS
I almost forgot to mention The Husband. The amazing, gorgeously wonderful force of positive energy that is Carson. Without your total belief in my capabilities, I would never have had the courage to share my work.

    Also, I'm rubbish with computers so without your patience and input none of this would be happening.

Huge thank you, darling Hub. xxx

INDEX

The Chocolate Cheesecake	1
Home Alone	3
The Secret Dinner Party Guest	6
The Diggers	8
Family Dog	10
Mylo	12
Guardian Angels	14
The Mask	17
Lady in Red	19
It's 2am	20
Grieving	22
I'd Like to Have a Dog Again	24
To Lizzie	25
The Dog from Dorset	28
I Love My Dog	30
My Dogs Have Developed a Worrying Trait	32
The Wolf in The Kitchen	35
When Evening Comes	37
Mollie Moo	39
Boris, The Terrier	41
Missing	43
The Obedience Challenge	45
Winning The Lottery	50
Barking The Boundaries	53
Dog Farts	54

This is How I Fell in Love	55
Newsflash	56
Bedlington Whippets	57
Animal Instincts	59
To Liam, This Life	61
The Phantom Dog Poo Bagger	64
Peter and Harvey,	
The Weimaraner Alias Smith & Jones	65
Lex, The Staffy	68
Who Dunnit?	71
We Are Waving	74
Reclaiming the Beach	76
Fudge, The Reading Companion	78
Grown Up	81
Friends Forever	83
Peggy, The Cocker Poo	85
Mabel	87
Don't Make Me Go to The Vets	88
Medication Mayhem	90

WHISKY AND BEARDS

THE CHOCOLATE CHEESECAKE

She stared at the empty pie plate,
a look of horror on her face.
Eyes wide, a mix of shock and wonder,
Oh my God! What a waste!

Once, there was a cheesecake,
made with tender, loving care
by this newly wed, so keen to impress
with her new found culinary flare.
Lovingly, she'd mixed icing sugar
with mascarpone cheese,
spread it upon a biscuit base,
and in her attempt to please
her guests, who were due to arrive
hungry, within the hour,
she placed it on a cut-glass stand,
decorated with flowers.

And then she made a big mistake,
distracted by the phone,
this kitchen goddess turned her back
and a canine Al Capone
leapt & seized his moment,
and in one tongue full, scoffed the lot;
slowly the horror dawned on her
that cheesecake was all she'd got.

There was no back up in the fridge,
no ice cream in the freezer,
to placate her guests, who knew her well,
and were all likely to tease her
if, they caught her, rushing out to find
the nearest cash dispenser,
hoping to buy a substitute
from a local Marks & Spencer.

If only she'd been more watchful,
placed the pud on a higher shelf.
Shut the wretched dog out of the kitchen.
Well, was no one to blame but herself.
And all the while the clock kept ticking,
forlornly, she held up a bag of chocolate chips.
As the precious whippet crept back to bed,
and quietly licked his lips.

HOME ALONE

Two little dogs were left alone,
with plenty of water, and a raw hide bone.
Their owners had gone for a good night out
to see a show, scream and shout.
They left them in the living room
with the promise that, *we'll be back soon,*
and though they were comfy on the settee,
their tummies rumbled. *What's for tea?*
The usual fare seemed quite humdrum,
neither of them fancied Pedigree Chum™.

Into the kitchen they shuffled on little fat bottoms,
only to discover the humans had forgotten
to close the door, where the food was kept.
So, into the pantry the pair of them crept.
They found potatoes tied in a bag,
and between the pair of them managed to drag
it into the middle of the kitchen floor,
played for a while, then went back for more.
They found carrots and onions tied up in sacks,
several ripe peaches, a box of flapjacks,
with a woof of delight, they gobbled them down,
now they were really going to town.

They'd got a taste for something sweet,
out flew a bag of sugar, a jar of mincemeat.
Luckily the jar wasn't broken,
but the sugar bag split, and soon burst open,
peppering the room, a snow-white shower,
the dogs went wild, found a bag of flour,
which they used to play a tug of war,
before adding the contents onto the floor.

A carton of orange juice hit the deck,
the lid flew off, it started to fleck
and splatter their faces. A tango tsunami.
The resulting sugar rush sent the dogs barmy.
They were having such fun, and in no time at all
spilled out of the kitchen and into the hall.
There, exhausted, they went off to sleep,
with a packet of biscuits and a pint of Black Sheep™.

The humans were shocked when they opened the door
found the ruffians sprawled on the floor.
Oh my God one of them gurgled.
Is it the dogs? Or have we been burgled?
No, it's our fault cried the other grabbing a broom.
We should've shut them out of the room.
Once we've cleared this mess, I shall need an analgesia!
The dogs opened their eyes, total amnesia.

Why on earth they wondered
did our humans make this mess?
We'd better comfort them. They look so distressed.
Soft, goo-goo eyes, a paw on a knee,
slow thump of the tail. *It couldn't possibly have been me.*
The humans, in evening dress, sank onto the rug,
burst out laughing, gave them a hug.

THE SECRET DINNER PARTY GUEST

The evening was a success, or so the hostess thought,
as her guests retired to the parlour,
to enjoy a glass of port.
Smiling, she listened to small talk,
The Turner Gallery in Margate,
while Lily, the Italian Greyhound,
silently tackled the child gate;
positioned in the doorway,
between the dining room and kitchen,
for the pickings on the table were delectable,
and rich in doggy delights; usually forbidden,
strictly taboo,
that naughty Lily couldn't resist; come on,
what's a dog to do?

Silently, on tippy-toes she jumped upon a chair,
from which the step to table, was simple,
climbing a stair.
Stealthily, commando like, she side stepped the cutlery,
to finish off the mille-feuille, so scrumptious and buttery.
Next, she tackled the side plates,
carefully licked them clean, she'd never imagined
so much food in all her doggie dreams.

Haughtily she paused, raised her head, sniffed the air.
What was that aroma? Ah, yes, stilton and pear,
there was the cheeseboard. How is a dog meant to resist?
So, she had a little nibble,
polished off the last Parmesan Twist.
The salty taste made her thirsty,
so she had a glass of wine,
that cheeky, red berry Merlot, utterly divine.
She tip-toed through champagne flutes,
having a sip from every one,
this really was the best banquet ever,
Lily was having such fun.

But she knew
it was high-time she returned to the kitchen,
thus ensuring, no one found out,
about her high life addiction.
Her owner took her up to bed once the last guest had left,
and in the duvet cuddled her tight,
knowing nothing of the theft.
'Though, when awoken at 3am
our hostess did think it funny,
that darling Lily kept breaking wind, and
had rather an upset tummy.

THE DIGGERS

Nellie and Lisa, whippets of perfection,
were shut in the lounge for their own protection.
Their owners went out, having foolishly decided
the two little darlings wouldn't be misguided
to do anything, remotely naughty.
Look at the pair of them. They just look so haughty.

For a while they sat, like works of art,
engrossed in the telly, heart to heart.
Until one of them noticed a mark on the sofa,
whilst practising Down Dog, a movement from yoga.
A tiny tear, revealing some fluff,
Lisa pulled with her teeth, and soon, sure enough
out came a wad of snow white flocking,
she coaxed out some more, with a bit of prodding
and help from Nellie, her partner in crime,
both tugged and pulled at the same time.
Soon the pile grew of the magical fluff,
the dogs were jubilant. *What is this stuff?*

A claw caught the fabric, the tear grew bigger,
the dogs went loopy, turned into diggers.
Nellie was certain she'd heard a squeak,
whilst pulling and stripping braid with her feet.
An invisible mouse sent the hounds
into a frenzy. *It must be found!*

Honed on their quarry, they went on a mission
to destroy the enemy, not a hint of contrition.
A shower of foam and fluff and dust,
littered the carpet. Still, needs must.
The imaginary rodent never did appear,
not that it mattered, that was clear.
It was just such enormous fun,
to dig up the sofa with a favourite chum.

Then, in the background, a key turned in a lock.
It was just enough to make the pair of them stop,
and return to sitting back in a pose
that just screamed decorum, apart from a nose
from which some fluff, hung from a whisker,
suggesting shenanigans staged by the sisters.
In the silence that followed, humans looked in dismay
at the hole in the sofa caused by the melee.
The whippets just stared, unabashed and diffident,
Don't know how that happened. We are totally innocent.

FAMILY DOG

Stately and sturdy, Ben's on guard,
protecting his family, a canine diehard.
Likeable and loyal, he lies in the lounge,
hoping for handouts, his nose on the scrounge.

This is his job, a fetcher and go for,
hanging with humans who slump on the sofa.
Eating their tissues when movies are tearful,
making them laugh, endearingly cheerful.
This family has his total affection,
and when he's without them, total dejection.

He waits by the door, stares through the glass,
barks at the postman, and any who pass
by the boundary, which he must defend,
from marauders, intruders, and the latest boyfriend.

Time ticks slowly till quarter past three,
when most of the family return for tea.
The front door slams, bags drop to the floor,
Ben goes potty, all snuffles and paws.
His family are home, his life is complete,
all troop to the kitchen, trip over his feet.

Kettles are boiled, sandwiches buttered,
wolfed from a table, messy and cluttered.
Hammering feet run up the stairs,
there's music and shouting, squeaking of chairs.

A teen in his bedroom, strums out a beat
with Ben for company, warming his feet.
Another is crying, Ben's at the door,
and anyone watching knows he adores
this human pack, who love him no end.
The family dog. The beautiful Ben.

MYLO

Mylo, black labradorable.
King of the sofa. First in line for scraps, which
for tummy's sake are few, but well worth a
High-5 paw exchange for tit-bits.

He's the holder of sleepover secrets,
whispered in chatterbox bedrooms
filled with music and mirth.
Sports antlers at Christmas,
daisy chains in Summer,
running through long grass with small people
chasing butterflies and bees.

Oversees the campervan Dad's
struggle to find room for bikes and balls
among the French-frames, bedding and booze.
Mylo's broad beam squeezes in with
hurray-for-the-holiday humans.
Sits beneath stars while
'Ride on Time' revellers re-live their youth
egged on by the young,
whose legs will grow longer by Autumn.

Mylo has taught them much
since the days of Jumping Jack shoes,
has soothed their tears,
seen the latest craze come and go.
Watched snowmen rise, then melt away.

Today, his ear flicks
as the taken-to-the-edge Mum
re-enforces boundaries to
temper flashing teens, who
can be both sweet pea and sulky simultaneously.

Lately, Mylo has taken to sleeping with
one eye open, primed for his next role in life.
It will be he who passes judgment
on teenage suitors who will soon
start flocking to the door.
For only those who receive
The Mylo Paw-of-Approval
will be allowed to stay for dinner.

GUARDIAN ANGELS

Yoda and Poppy, just two dogs, ordinary family pets,
no one knew what the future held,
or how much they'd be in their debt.

Until the day that someone died, Peter,
a husband and a dad,
his motorbike in the garage, his writing on a pad,
dirty clothes in the washing, a novel left unread,
an empty chair at the table, and an ache in the bed.

Yoda sat on the driveway, his human hadn't come back.
Poppy hid in her basket,
afraid of the strangers dressed in black.
Once they left,
dust fell slowly onto a silence filled with sound,
Poppy came out of hiding, Yoda returned and found
their family torn to pieces, fragmented by their grief,
the illusion of stability stolen,
by the Grim Reaper's thief.
Everyone was talking, yet no one said the word,
the future mouthed frantically, unable to be heard.

No one noticed the dogs
as they padded around the house,
watching the boy without a father,
the wife without a spouse.
But, whenever they found someone crying,
the dogs were right there with a paw,
to touch a hand, a knee, whatever it took,
to help the humans they adored.
They'd wrap themselves around
whoever lay sobbing on the bed,
and everyone found comfort,
as they gently stroked their heads.

Although, at times it was hard
to have to take them for a walk,
it made the family go out together,
spend time, simply talk.
Yes, there was a hole.
No, life wouldn't be the same.
But they still had each other.
No one was to blame.
Reality reached out her arms,
Peter's role in life was brief,
everything has a polarity,
the yang to love,
is grief.

But, having the dogs for company,
helped the pain to ease,
and the touch of a cold nose
allowed joy to gently tease
a smile, some respite;
it was still fun in the park.
As the dogs often reminded them,
every time they watched them bark at
falling leaves, invisible monsters, chasing birds,
or simply for fun.
Those angels healed a family,
just by being there.

Job well done.

THE MASK

He sits alone on a paint peeled bench,
dirty hands, with fists that clench.
Unkept hair, unwashed, defiant,
a towering, hostile, unshaven giant.

Passers hurry the other way,
avoiding the face, etched in clay.
He looks the sort who'd start a fight,
one to avoid on a cold dark night.

One soul hides behind park gate and
peeps at the face engraved with hate.
Watches the man, alone at last,
waits to see him remove the mask.

Sees the hate just slip away.
Sees the hands that start to play
with the ears of a little dog, by his side.
Sees the eyes now soft with pride.

Yes, here's a man with a chequered past.
who hides behind a hostile mask.
His mind a tortured battlefield, but
with his dog, his true self is revealed.

The soul that watches, sees the man.
The real one. The one no one else can.
The one now gazing down from above,
who smiles at his dog, and reveals true love.

LADY IN THE RED

She still walks you know,
the lady whose dog died.
I see her from my window,
that purposeful stride.
A bright red anorak,
punctuates the mist,
just, minus the lead,
cradled in her fist.

We spoke the other day,
and a tear escaped
as we embraced each other,
our arms a cape,
remembering her dog,
he was nervous, but jolly.
I don't know her name,
but I knew her collie.

IT'S 2am

It's 2am.
I'm standing on the lawn,
barefoot, faded dressing gown, looking for you.
You, busy, snuffling about in the bushes.
Your beard appears, tinged silver by the moonlight.
Trotting back towards the kitchen
your diva paws dance across the stepping stones.
You don't acknowledge me.
Not even a backward glance
as you pass, muttering
Look up. See the stars. Aren't they beautiful?

It's 2am.
I'm asleep.
Well, pretending to be,
while you, my magnificent husband
escort The Precious down the stairs,
her bladder isn't what it was.
I don't have to be watching to know
you'll wait patiently by the back door
while Herself is busy outside
hunting for the best place
to curtsey. I know
when she finally returns
you'll raise an eyebrow as
she toddles past, shake your head and smile.
So patient. So wonderful.
My giant of a man

It's 2am.
I'm in the garden.
But you're not here.
No diva paws dancing
on stepping stones tonight.
The sky is cloudy and
there are no stars.
But, it is still beautiful.
I don't need to see the stars
to know they are there.
I hope you are well pleased
with your student.

Good bye Fidget.
My teacher and friend.
My shining star.

GRIEVING

I wish I had a Tardis
so I could fly into a colour photograph of you.
You on the lawn in meditative form,
contemplating the sun.
And everything would be as it was,
because, you gave my life meaning
and now I am reeling because you've left.
Bereft of your guidance, I curl here in silence
and disappear.

Hot tears,
splatter my face and chase each other to my chin.
My head is aching while this body is breaking
with grief. And there is no relief,
your memory litters my house.
There's your lead in the hall and
in the corner your ball, battered and chewed.
A dog bed on the landing and from where I am standing
your head used to peep from the rug.
Now, it's devoid of your hairs,
and the stairs don't need sweeping, so
why do the housekeeping,
when there's no one making a mess.

I press your collar in my hand and
this tiny band of leather is all I have left.
While the theft of The Reaper
cuts my heart deeper,
I knew this day would come.
Yet, still I succumbed to your charm.

This is love.
These tears, this face, a red eyed disgrace.
But none of it a waste.
I gave you unconditional love knowing
you would die, and while I am grieving
I am also perceiving that this pain
is the yang to love, and above all else
I'm glad my heart can feel it.

I was enthralled by your frantic, hole digging antics
you could change my mood just by cocking your head.
I know it's absurd,
but I don't miss the turd in my pocket.
Oh, stop it.
Look what you've done.
There's laughter and sadness,
this is madness,
I feel them both intertwined.
And so, I am able to find peace.
Well, in this moment at least.

I'D LIKE TO HAVE A DOG AGAIN

I'd like to have a dog again,
a companion, to go for a walk
and all I ask is that she's faithful and
will listen when I talk.
That she'll look to my face,
wrinkle her brow as if she's really listening,
and she'll come to me eyes shining,
as soon as she hears me whistling.

I really want another dog,
for I miss that warm caress
when my hand strokes her flank,
and I can feel her take a breath.
I want my face to be buried
in her wonderfully smelly ruff,
and I want to curl a twill
on her woolly forehead tuft.

My life feels empty
without a dog for when I close the door
the silence pulls me downward,
I want someone to care for.
Someone to come home to,
who'll greet me at my feet,
a dog to share my life with,
so I can feel complete.

TO LIZZIE

I'm glad I'm supple,
so I can sit on the floor
with my legs crossed in awkward places.
My face is captured
by the being nestled in my arms.
You have tiny feet, and
peep through eyes so misted
you can barely see, and
it pleases me just to have you near.

You peer at my hands,
suckle a finger, teeth like needles,
while I just linger.
Lost in the moment.
Caught up in your spell.
You smell of
sweetness and milk
as I raise you up and
gently tilt your face to mine.
Sublime.

My eyes see a friend
sharing walks on hills,
me wearing mittens against Winter chills
while you dance
across frozen puddles.

We'll huddle by fires,
me clutching a mug of dark,
hot chocolate, and
your tail will thud, begging biscuits,
while we watch Strictly on the telly.

Your belly will wobble
when you squirm on your back, and
lying in the bed I'll come under attack
from your whiskers,
buried in my face.

You'll be the disgrace of the class,
when you run off barking,
ignoring The Stay,
instead you'll come prancing,
chasing your human when my back is turned,
but I won't care because
I'll never spurn your love.

Teach me to smile at the hurly burly life with a dog
never surly with the gargoyle
clutching my shoe in her lips, as
I wrestle to retrieve it, fingertips dripping with drool.

Destroy my garden.
Dig up the lawn.
Leave my cushions battered and torn.
Knock me sideways when you run up the stairs.
Cover my carpets in dust and hair.
Leave your pawprints everywhere.

And then grow old.

Be fifteen or more with white eyebrows,
and a bladder that is unreliable.
Disturb my sleep.
Get me up in the dark.
Take an hour just to toddle round the park,
because once you are deaf
and there is nothing to see, then
sniffing a tree will be ecstasy.

Grow old.
Grow very, very old.
Grow old,
with me.

THE DOG FROM DORSET

Because you came from Dorset,
full of sass, with teeth like needles,
but I was still in love
with the ashes in the cabinet next to my bed,
we didn't get on.
She'd said. *Are you, my Mummy?*
And I'd replied. *Yes, I will always be your Mummy.*
But when I told you *I'm your Mum.*
You went *whatever*
then stalked off with my slipper in your mouth.

You didn't walk to heel, you hung off my trouser leg,
and when my hand stroked your nose,
you chose to draw blood from my finger.
My guests were your giant dog toys,
swinging from their hair was one of your joys.
No wonder people stopped coming.
I spent a fortune on food.
The best organic cuts of meat,
designer mixes and chickens' feet
none of which met with your approval.
I thought you were just awkward,
wished I'd never driven down the A303.
You cocked you head and
said to me *you need to learn. I'm not her.*

Oh, I cried and sulked, wished things were different,
that you looked like her,
and weren't indifferent to my attempts at affection.
You shared my home but, gave me no respect.
Funny thing, once I stopped comparing you to a ghost,
worked with what I'd got, rather than what I wanted,
I felt the shift.

The best part of my day is at 5am.
You join me on the bed, stretch out your legs,
rest your head on my chest, listening to my heart.
I lie with you on one side, and
her ashes in the cabinet
on the other.

You're not her.

She died in May.

But it's alright.
I'm getting used to that.

I LOVE MY DOG

I love my dog.
Not when the sun shines,
but when she finds my hand in the rain.
When my automatic step holds no delight,
I see the flashlight on her collar
I holla her to come, and
she runs straight to me in the dark.

I love my dog.
Not in the Down, Sit or Stay
but in the way she looks sideways
when she steals my glove.
It matters not her breed or colour of her coat,
I love to find her stray hairs
in the back of my throat when we play.

Now, this dog plays rough,
she nips my nose, but I chose
to have a dog that is feisty.
One minute she's all bitey,
the next, she has her head on my lap,
I chat to her about my day and she says
nothing.

I don't speak Woof.
She doesn't speak Human.
That doesn't matter, because
we use intuition to communicate.
She feels my mood.

On days when I sit
in a round shouldered chair,
she's there, snuffling,
rubbing her face against mine.
And I'm glad my dog chose
my nose to nip.
Her teeth hurt.
I love it.

MY DOGS HAVE DEVELOPED A WORRYING TRAIT

My dogs have developed a worrying trait.
I taught them some tricks, I thought it was great
to watch them perform for my entertainment.
But now it appears this type of arrangement
has gone awry; this learning spree
has totally backfired, they're training me.

I taught them to fetch, and now they insist
I continue to throw till I'm dismissed.
They stop the game, go off in a huff
for a new kind of fun and, oddly enough
they find the smell at the base of a tree,
a lot more exciting than little old me.

They dictate the pace when we're out for a walk,
I can scarcely breathe, let alone talk.
Rope burns scar my blistered hands
as I'm dragged along by this motley band,
who give chase to anything fluffy that wiggles,
furtive cats, nut thieving squirrels.

I wanted their diet to be tasty, nutritious,
the blurb on the packet said wholesome, delicious.
Yet it failed to meet with their expectations,
caused a breakdown in happy relations.
They got together and decided instead
to stage a protest, refuse to be fed.

So, it's chaos at mealtimes, totally manic,
noses are turned, if I don't serve organic.
Their moods and whims are driving me crazy,
insisting on rice and chicken jalfrezi.
I thought all dogs just ate from a tin,
you wouldn't believe the mess I'm in.

Bloomin' dogs, they're so demanding,
the pitch of the woof, pertinent, commanding.
I plump up their cushions, make sure they're comfy,
buy chews and treats that are tasty and crunchy.
I pick up their poos, all soggy and whiffy.
I'm not their owner, I'm just their skivvy.

I was firm in the beginning, no dogs upstairs.
But then, one night I was caught unawares.
It was dark and stormy, thunder and lightning,
the little darlings all claimed it was frightening.
Come share my duvet I foolishly said,
now they've moved in, taken over my bed.

The living room furniture's covered in throws,
I need hardly explain, you can guess how it goes.
No dogs on the sofas that's what I said,
then spent a fortune on baskets and beds.
So, how come it's me who's sat on the rug,
while they're on the settee, all smiley and smug?

Here on the floor, life's not without risk,
they drink my wine and steal my crisps.
Suck me in with seal like eyes.
Well look out dogs, I'm getting wise.
You don't fool me with your Battersea looks.
I know the truth. You're a bunch of crooks!

You've ransacked my wardrobe, wrecked all my clothes,
I used to be smart, now anything goes.
Whatever I'm wearing, it's covered in hair,
and do you know what, I really don't care.
Ok, I moan, sometimes I'm crabby,
but living with dogs, just makes me happy.

The smell's delicious when their coats are all wet.
Paw prints are tiresome I know, and yet
just the sight of the eyes and the beard,
something happens, it's totally weird.
None of it matters, not the hassle or the stains.
I'm proud to announce, I am totally dog trained.

THE WOLF IN THE KITCHEN

Dylan is waiting,
waiting for something to happen,
for something to happen to drop on the floor.

Opens a door, sneaks under the table
protected by long socks and small shoes.
Hoovers up a discarded chip,
a stray baked bean, unseen by Grandad
creator of sausage wigwams and
fishfinger volcanoes.

Distracted by skillet and spoon
he chooses to ignore the paw,
and the ketchup fingers
dropping booty
to be gorged upon
by this gorgeous one,
who retrieves balls and lost slippers,
comes to the call of warbling whistlers,
romps on the floor with wiggling gigglers
depositing hair on school skirts and
trouser legs.

They say he is descended from
wolves, scavenging scraps of meat
by moonlight near the fire.

Today, this 'wolf' is snuggled on
the sofa watching CBBC and
the only trace of his ancestry
is a razor sharp reaction towards
unattended food.

Dylan is waiting,
waiting for something to happen,
for something to happen to drop on the floor.
So he can gnaw on it, and pretend
just for a moment,
that he is still
a wolf.

WHEN EVENING COMES

When evening comes, out goes the light,
I sink into the duvet and squeeze up tight to my humans,
who can hardly move, turn over easily, or even use
their pillows.
You see,
I must rest my head on that billowy softness,
that feathery bed.

I have to say
the humans I adore are a bit of a pain,
nightmare when they snore.
You see, a dog like me needs room for legs
to stretch out long, and occasionally begs and pushes
for that extra room, thus separating my humans
asleep in their tomb.

Quietly I shove and kick a bit more,
till eventually one of them lands on the floor.
I know! You'd think I'd get kicked off the bed.
But, my humans, they love me, it has to be said.
No one will banish me down the hall.
Instead one will curl me up a ball,
climb back into the marriage bed,
kiss me softly
on top of my head.

I know I'm pushy.
I know I shouldn't shove
my humans, whom I truly love.
I know they love me, and feel the same,
and it's not my fault
I was born a Great Dane.

MOLLIE MOO

Appearing to be asleep, by the window near the loo,
lies the ace secret assassin, malicious Mollie Moo.
Her eyes swivel constantly,
like someone watching tennis,
just waiting for the postman, that evil strutting menace.

A crunch on the gravel, Mollie's ear gives half a flick
she flies down the hallway, before a toc becomes a tic.
Hairy feet scrabble and scuff the parquet floor,
screaming like a banshee she assaults the oak front door.
A Valkyrie in meltdown, instantaneous combustion
she's a canine whirling dervish,
a weapon of 'male' destruction.

Her head pokes from the cat flap,
a yapping jaw with eyes
while the poor unfortunate postman in a blind panic tries
to thrust a handful of letters through the flapping box,
while the snarling little cairn,
gives it large with all she's got.

As the spit and saliva splatters
down the poor man's shin,
Mollie Moo's owner simply ignores the din.

All this talk of an 'evil' dog, is surely said in jest,
for her human truly believes her life is greatly blessed
by a doting, faithful companion, so gentle and polite,
she'd blanch at the notion;
precious Mollie would never bite.
Look at that tiny face, aren't those eyebrows beautiful?
She always comes to call.
Well, almost. Yes, she's dutiful.

She really is Miss Perfect,
ideal around the house.
Watch her trot into the kitchen,
waving letters in her mouth.
Sit patiently by the table, awaiting a meaty treat,
before nodding off quietly by her loving owner's feet.

The postie limps away, trembling and distressed,
Molly curls a lip,
come tomorrow, be my guest.
Her covert behaviour, seeks deliberately to misguide,
Magnificent Mollie Moo.
A canine Jekyll and Hyde.

BORIS, THE TERRIER

Boris, is a terrier, with a reputation to be feared,
he's bold, tenacious, just a tad weird.
When he spots a dog on the other side of the street,
his first response is gushing, rushing over to meet
his new four-legged chum, all lofty, bombastic,
his stumpy tail wags, just so enthusiastic.

Then, he remembers he follows The Code,
nobodies' pet, he's in hostile dog mode.
Snuffles and growls, strains at the lead,
full of aggression he snaps, and proceeds
to drag his poor owner towards the fray,
while everyone simply looks on in dismay.

Who is this gremlin? This black-eyed brute.
Moments ago, he just looked so cute.
Now he's a salivating, fiend with fangs,
with a trembling human who frantically hangs
onto the leash, trying hard not to trip,
get caught up in brambles, or lose her grip.

Then, Boris spies a bicycle wheel,
plunging forward, he starts to squeal,
runs after the cyclist at world record pace,
his unfortunate owner also gives chase.

Boris, Boris! Leave! She cries, as
the lactic burns in the cyclist's thighs.
Boris himself, won't be outdone,
chasing bicycles is his kind of fun.

Spitting gravel, the tyres spin.
The bike chase Olympics!
Who's gonna win?
The panting cyclist cranks the gears,
the gap widens and he disappears
over the hill, Boris in tow.
Plus a panicking owner, who just won't let go.

Gobsmacked, spectators watch in awe
of the valiant lady, whose dog ignores her.
Boris, Boris! Please, please stop!
She gasps, and heaves with all she's got.
Her shoe flies off.
Her tights are laddered.
Handbag flapping, her face is battered,
lungs a' bursting, skin's a' glistening.
But she talks to the paw
'coz the face ain't listening!

MISSING

A daydreaming hiker left an open, swinging gate.
I should've gone and checked it,
now it's too late.
A sea of sulphurous rape, camouflages all,
my voice, drowned by the motorway,
struggles as I call *Fidget, where are you?*

Is she hiding under the green?
Chasing invisible bunnies,
scampering about unseen.
Or locked onto her quarry,
heading for the road.
My ears are ringing danger.
My limbs grow weak and cold.
Fidget, where are you?

Please. Please. Please, come back.
There's a Reaper hanging in the sky,
a raven dressed in black.
The snatching wind pulls my hair,
chokes me when I shout.
I see the posters MISSING
In a panic, I cry out
Fidget, where are you?

Please. Please. No, I plead.
I wish I'd never come here,
never let you off the lead.
Look at me just standing here
like a half dead windswept tree, and
there's no one else to blame,
just stupid careless me
Oh, Fidget, where are you?

Stumbling,
I turn,
trip, nearly fall, and
there she is, behind me,
answering my call. Me,
a hammer in my head,
body locked and tense.
Fidget's tail, gesturing
from the other side of the fence.
Resting on her haunches,
like a yogi in a lotus.
Never lost at all, just
waiting to be noticed.

THE OBEDIENCE CHALLENGE

Reggie sat in silence,
to one side of the line,
patiently awaiting the off, his allotted starting time.
Bess the Border shook,
keen as mustard to have a go.
While Ellie barked,
ears pricked *I'm ready, don't you know*.

The task to perform was easy,
come when your handler calls,
ignoring all distractions, biscuits, toys and balls.
One by one competitors went with
varying degrees of success.
Until now, with only three to go,
the next one up, was Bess.
Padding her paws, she quivered,
head down, between the cones,
no way she'd be distracted,
this dog was in The Zone.
She hurtled like a meteor
the minute her owner beckoned,
smashed the time to take the lead,
in under sixty five seconds.

Next, it was Ellie's turn,
paws placed behind the line,
she got off well, bang on course to complete
in record time.
But her eyes wandered for a moment,
beckoned by a Kong.
She couldn't resist a little play.
So, now her chance had gone.
A high-pitched voice shouted,
Ellie Belly! Come to me!
She left the toy and passed the post,
in one minute, twenty-three.

Last to go was Reggie,
the competition was his, providing
he did the recall without getting in a tizz.
He kept one eye on his owner,
the one he ought to please,
the other scoured the distractions.
The toys. The food. The cheese.
A tiny glob of saliva,
dribbled down his chest, this task was
his nemesis, a concentration test.
Could he keep his focus?
Simply run down the track,
ignoring those tempting goodies,
once his owner called him back.

With a flourish, the flag was lowered,
the crowd, forward in their seats,
his owner started praying,
please let him ignore the treats.
But only two strides later,
a Boneo called his name, and
not to crunch this yummy snack
would've simply been a shame.
You see, Reggie was a Retriever,
food was his Big Thing,
unable to resist a tempting treat,
he was never going to be thin.

After eating the biscuit, he copped a bowl of chicken,
wolfed it down in seconds, gave his lips a licking.
Reggie! A voice shouted. The dog responded.
Oh, good boy! and
ran straight past the following test,
a fluffy, squeaky toy.
Stopping abruptly, he turned around,
went back from whence he came,
deciding to bring it with him,
surely, part of the fun and games.
Leave! his owner roared.
Reg dropped it from his lips,
only to be distracted again.
What's that? A bag of chips?

Actually, they were carrots,
Reggie ate them, everyone laughed.
Then he lolloped a few more feet then stopped,
licked his arse.
Scratched his belly, rubbed an ear,
stood up, cocked a leg.
All the crowd went potty when
he ran off with an egg.

The growling judge however,
was really not amused,
I think you'd better fetch your dog.
I want that reprobate removed.
Red faced, the owner walked the plank,
the green lawn of doom,
rounded shoulders, lowered face,
a perfect picture of gloom.

He wished he'd bought a different dog.
A collie. A big Alsatian.
But one by one the audience rose,
gave him a standing ovation.
For they saw a beautiful retriever,
aiming simply to please, go and
sit before his owner,
tail wagging *Yes, it's me.*

They cheered watching young man's face
break into the widest, biggest grin,
knowing it really didn't matter,
Reg was never going to win.

Later in the evening, after a
nice soak in the bath, this
human and his companion finally
had a chance to curl up
together on a sofa past its best
and put behind them the nemesis of
the concentration test.

See, there's more to life than accolades,
trophies and rosettes, because
Reggie's was the performance
the crowd all loved the best.

WINNING THE LOTTERY

Sometimes, I wish,
I hope I'll win the lottery.
Have loads of money, go
buy all the things I want.
But, not today.

Today, longline limp in my hand,
I handed you an opportunity,
trusted you.
You have to, sometimes.
Sometimes you have to test,
to trust the training.

I let you loose.

Ears down, you trotted
by my feet on the headland.
I smiled at your
grasshopper high surprise when you
thought you'd found a vole.
It was just a leaf.
Relieved you were calm, I
started to relax, catch a bit of sun,
noticed someone had strolled here earlier,
left their tracks in the dew.

You, snorting and snuffling
caught their scent. Went from laid-back lurcher
to scud missile in a heartbeat.
My heart, beating out a morse code
loaded with remorse. How stupid.
Of course, you'd run off.

Helpless,
I watched your turkey drumstick
thighs pump, piston like
into the distance.
Standing, lonely as a tree,
I wondered.
Will you come back when I call?
All that training, now on trial.
Fingers shaking, I fumbled for the
whistle round my neck,
put it to my lips.

Whistled.

Paused.

Whistled again.

Then, watched, mouth open in awe.

You stopped.
Turned around and ran
towards me,
eyes shining at the fun of it all.

Galloping too fast to stop,
you overshot,
circled back, slapped
my leg with your tail and
sat.

Smiling,
I cupped your face in my hands
kissed your nose,
gave you a treat.

Sometimes, I wish
I hope I'll win the lottery.
Today, I did.
The dice fell in my favour,
giving me everything I could
ever wish for, and
so much more.

Such a relief.

BARKING THE BOUNDARIES

Yogi's always barking,
he does it night and day at monsters in the garden
he has to have his say.
Tail up, ears pricked,
Napoleon of aggression,
chasing cats and birds is his hobby, and obsession.
'Click,' goes the kitchen door,
a frenzied fiend of fur shoots off up the garden,
little legs a blur.
Bang! He hits the boundary fence
with paws like fists, he pounds,
then struts around the fish pond,
patrolling all his grounds.
His voice, it carries far and wide in the neighbourhood,
Oy, you intruders. You're not welcome, understood?!
Beady eyes that burn, full of fury, and hate,
at all who seek to avoid the hound at the gate.
Lips curl, teeth bared,
you'd better run and cower,
If you know what's good for you.
Don't mess wif a chihuahua!

DOG FARTS

My eyes are starting to water,
something's catching in my throat,
the goldfish in the aquarium have all begun to float.
The flowers are all wilting on my continental quilt,
and the coffee in my mug has slowly turned to silt.

Who was the comedian who let him up here on the bed?
After eating those rotting apples,
and that rabbit that was dead.
We're going to have to muzzle him
when we go out for a walk,
he's a guzzler on the lookout,
whether it squeaks or it squawks.
Live or inert, it's always worth a chew,
an old discarded glove, another dog's spew.
Slowly his tummy processes this cocktail of delights,
a bogey sodden hanky, a pair of smelly tights.

It doesn't seem to bother him, but it really bothers me,
the air's so thick and cloudy now, I can barely see.
He lies there unrepentant, totally comatose,
his own smell doesn't register in that great big soppy nose.
He sleeps, eyes firmly shut, head covered with a paw,
but this is what it's like to live with an ageing Labrador.

THIS IS HOW I FELL IN LOVE

This is how I fell in love.

I never wanted to have a dog.
I never wanted to have a dog.

With all the hassle and hairs,
the have to take it for a walk.
Talk about commitment.
Talk about commitment.

I've got all the worry empathy brings,
all the what ifs.
Like, what if she gets stolen, lost or sick.

But I don't think of that on the sofa,
among the cushions and throws,
her nose on my lap.

This is where I am happiest.
This is where I fell in love.

NEWSFLASH

I was trying to read the newspaper
until you came along,
jumped on the sofa,
smashed your paws on the headlines.

The red top disappeared,
my only view was you,
magnificent eyebrows,
mouth open in a grin.

You rolled
across my knees and onto your back,
Brexit et al was squashed flat.
You asked a question
Cuddles or current affairs?

No Contest.
How could I resist.

BEDLINGTON WHIPPETS

I love lurchers.
I love little lurchers.
Little lurchers with beards
who think it is weird to go out in the rain.
Who blame a soaking proximity
for their inability to leave the sofa.

They lounge around, pretending to sleep,
peep from eyelids
heavy from doing nothing.
Yawn, without bothering to raise their heads,
they have no intention of quitting their beds,
not even for a quick trip outside to the loo.

Cast iron bladders
hang on through hailstorms and thunder.
They know if they lie with hips fully flexed,
they won't even notice,
let alone become vexed by
pressure on the pelvic floor.
Which anyway, can easily be ignored
if distracted by the duvet.

Lurchers are very wise.
They know eventually everything comes to an end,
even the rain. So,
they're content to watch from the window
until it's over. Dismiss
the growl from the bowel
till convenient to pop out for relief
which for all its importance,
will undoubtedly be brief.
They'll soon be crashed back on the bed
pressed like limpets against my leg.
Ensuring I stop doing
all the things that need doing
that really don't need doing at all.

So much better to sprawl
with the long dogs on a Sunday morning.
Treasure some leisure time together,
caressing rough coats and
soft ears, listening to the rain
tapping on the window.

ANIMAL INSTINCT

My Little Pony
is pulling my arms from their sockets.

The woods are alive with squirrels,
some harvesting their hard-earned hoard
of nuts. Others, the thieves
are bent on swooping down from above
sweeping swathes of leaves into spirals.
Together they wrestle,
a frenzied tangle of tails and teeth.

A dog trainer might say
exert control, make her walk to heel.
But, I know a lost cause when I see one, and
anyway you are alive with the fun of it all
anticipating the chase you must never have.

You are a sighthound
being a sighthound.
Across the road
there are squirrels,
being squirrels.
All of you oblivious to danger.

Tufty's neck will snap with one bite of your jaw.
Your long dog skull will splinter if
you run into the trunk of a tree.
Or the front of a car.

Squealing your frustration,
you call me a kill-joy.

You have no idea,
just how often I save your life.

TO LIAM, THIS LIFE

It's so short,
this life. I watch
you gallop, cornering at speed
sending dewdrops flying
into the sun.

I stand,
your leash, limp in my hand,
mesmerised by
your magnificence,
your athleticism
unhindered by constraint.

You run,
just for the fun of it.
Then, stop,
tongue lolling from your black lips,
hideously beautiful.

You are beautiful
in your wildness.
Flanks heaving,
eyes that belong
to no one.

Then, without a care
you roll in something
foul to me,
heavenly to you.
Flip,
from one side to the other.

I should stop you.
Should stop you?
Why?
How can I?
Your life is so short.
Why waste precious
moments on a scolding.

You are full of
the joy of knowing,
of being alive.

What is this life, if
it is wasted with
not knowing how to feel?

Once you are finished.
When your dance is done,
you drop your ears
return to where I stand,
your head covered in
something vile, to me,
delightful, to you.

Together,
we drive home,
windows open.

Both of us joyful,
for different reasons.

THE PHANTOM DOG POO BAGGER

You see them dotted everywhere, parks streets or verge,
whether you walk in town or countryside,
your local nature reserve.
Neatly tied in coloured plastic,
an offering from a tail wagger
left by that elusive species,
The Phantom Dog Poo Bagger.

I've never seen one being dropped by
that sneaky litter lout
who can't be bothered to find a bin or carry it about.
The perpetrator's devoid of conscious,
or they wouldn't act the way they do,
after going to all that trouble and
bagging the offending poo.

Once they've scrapped it up, I wonder,
do they stand up, then drop it down?
Or pretend that they've forgotten it and
leave it on the ground.
Does this environmental vandal fling it high,
hoping no one will see?

And do they think *not my problem*, when
it ends up in a tree?

PETER & HARVEY, THE WEIMARANER. ALIAS SMITH & JONES

Harvey,
complex, silver ghost, most adept
at obedience training.
Model of maturity,
top-notch security for the family.
Loyal. Dependable. Steadfast.
And yet,
he is also a thief, sneaked from the kitchen
a joint of beef from the table.

The Sunday roast left to rest, guests distracted by
Lovely to see you. How long has it been?
Nobody noticed, the crime unseen, except by Peter,
the generous host.
In a most laid-back tone,
he quipped *Just checking the veg,*
before nipping outside to the hawthorn hedge,
where Harvey was about to devour his prize,
grabbing his collar Peter managed to prise
the joint from the jaws of the tricksy thief.
Give it back. Villainous beast!

Luckily the meat was still intact.
Infact no one would know
if it wasn't for the
glowing glob of saliva dripping from the string.
Poor Peter. What a dilemma he was in.
What should he do? Cancel dinner?
Let everyone know what an
artful sinner the highly trained Harvey really was?
Because, the other option...

The other option was the one he preferred.

No one had seen, nobody'd heard a thing.
Admittedly, there was a moment of regret, and yet,
once the idea was hatched,
Peter rolled up his sleeves, no turning back.
The meat was washed under the tap,
wrapped in foil and quickly put back
to re-heat in the oven at Gas Mark 4,
Harvey dumped outside before closing the door,
very firmly.

The guests were chirpy after lunch,
oblivious to the anarchy, panicky panto and
the part Peter played in rescuing the feast.
The crunch of the roasties, simply divine.
All hail to the chef, that meat was sublime.
It was hard for Peter to keep his twitching face straight.
Sorry for the hold up, oven's not great, he said
tongue in cheek spreading the lie, glancing at Harvey
who he swore winked an eye.

Peter and Harvey.
Alias Smith & Jones.
Models of maturity,
top-notch security for the family.
Loyal. Dependable. Steadfast.
And yet,
the pair share a secret, it pains me to repeat.
One's prone to thievery,
the other, deceit.

LEX, THE STAFFY

Lex is The Boss.
This staffy is sassy and strong,
likes a ding-dong murder-thon with her toys.
Squirmy, wormy, smiley and wily
coming to call, extremely unlikely, unless
you have a meaty treat.
Stocky, stroppy, manipulative and soppy
she's the nose in the mug stealing your coffee.
And, she'll nick your biscuit,
if you glance the other way.

Lex isn't brave,
but, she is fearless when it comes to water.
The stalker of gulls on Winter beaches,
dives in the foam hunting her ball.
Rolls in the sand, barks at the waves,
plays dead,
when it's time to go home.

She can be obstinate.
You'll need to step across her
prostrate form to get to the door.
This lady's not for moving.

Possessive too,
try getting your slippers back.
She'd never bite the postman.
She will chase your cat, but,
it'll always get away.
Like I say, she's not brave.
That ginger-ninja was scary,
he hissed, had claws.

The top of the sofa is out of bounds,
technically.
Lex thinks her humans don't know
she's been peering out the window
while they're gone. Moon-eyed,
she tries to jump down
quick when the car comes back, but
that old cruciate scar slows her up.
She used to be such a power-packed pup,
still is, in short bursts.
Nowadays, snoozing in the sun
comes first on her to-do list.

She's more patient now.
Likes a belly rub and cuddle,
snuggled in her 'blankey' watching telly,
breath's a bit smelly,
toffee coloured coat flecked with grey.

Stills plays with the grandkids,
toddles behind them hoping for scraps.
Yaps, at the doorbell,
even though she's deaf,
allegedly.

She's had the most wonderful
harum-scarum life. Possibly
the most photographed dog on Facebook.
There may be others, equally indulged but,
none who are loved more.

She'll always be The Boss,
but no one seems to mind.

WHO DUNNIT?

A theft has been discovered, call in Scotland Yard, plus
a scientific forensic team with letters on their card.
Show them all the evidence, a tacky,
tongue smeared plate
plus, an empty mug of decaff, made with coffee mate.
Who nicked my elevenses? I'm sure there was a cake,
whoever's gone and gobbled it, has made a big mistake.

The perpetrator's fled the scene,
must have gone to ground.
Meanwhile, curled up in the corner,
quietly sleeps the hound.

The bedroom has been vandalised.
Where's Inspector Morse?
Or the DI from Shetland with his trusty Highland force.
Who dug up the duvet, shredded a box of tissues?
Cushions have been scattered,
the vandal must have issues.
Someone mullered a magazine, left it all in tatters.
Really, it's outrageous.
Did the headlines drive them crackers?

The delinquent has absconded,
left the battleground.
Meanwhile, curled up in the corner,
quietly sleeps the hound.

You there, get to Baker Street, go find Sherlock Holmes.
I cannot find my scrunchy, hairbrush or my comb.
They should be in my handbag.
But here's what's really cranky,
my purse has not been stolen,
just my lipstick and my hanky.
So, is our culprit super vain, with a snotty, runny nose?
Of course, I'm generalising. Truth is, no one knows.

The bandit's really cunning though,
left without a sound.
Meanwhile, curled up in the corner,
quietly sleeps the hound.

Oh, I'm getting fed-up now.
Have you seen my knickers?
I left them in the bathroom with
my posh socks and my slippers.
We need a trusted Super Sleuth to help with this debacle.
Excuse me Agatha Christie,
could you lend us old Miss Marple?
Jeez, it's so annoying, there'll soon be nothing left
I need to get a grip on this, the latest household theft.

But, no one witnessed anything,
when I asked around.
Meanwhile, curled up in the corner,
quietly sleeps the hound.

At last there's been a breakthrough,
someone's left a print.
A rather muddy paw and claw, now that must be a hint.
Ann Cleeves has lent us Vera,
now that's fair champion pet.
Our Geordie lass is nobbut canny,
she'll get the reiver yet.
The tracks all lead to the dog bed,
and there, gooey and manky
lie all the stolen booty, plus my knickers and my hanky.

It's a fair cop guv, we've got him,
the culprit has been found
snoring in his basket,
Dunnit the Basset Hound.

WE ARE WAVING

We are waving
to you with our ears,
running in circles,
chasing each other's tail.

We must seem small
to you from way up there
so busy in your loneliness.
Your minds are scattered
like the grains of sand
whipping across the beach.

Down here
the sun is kind,
we are having fun.

Do you miss
the kiss of the seasons?
Do you even notice their passing,
held captive as you are
by technology,
running apps, Facebook posts?

Most of our time
is spent hunting treasure,
rotting seaweed,
a discarded shoe.
What do you treasure?
What would you miss
if it wasn't here?

And
will you realise its value
before it is
too late?

RECLAIMING THE BEACH

After the rush,
once the schools have gone back,
and the beach huts are empty cause
it's too cold for bucket and spade,
the shoreline's reclaimed.

Dogs, gallop across wet sand, still ridged
by the tide. Dive after balls thrown in the foam
by puffa-coat humans sporting hats. Some dogs,
the acrobats, punctuate the air
claiming frisbees as their prize.
Others hide behind breakwaters
ready to pounce on the unwary.
Old friendships are re-kindled,
new buddies found foraging for treasure
in the shelter of chalk cliffs.

In this, the season of
drippy noses and frozen feet,
stoic souls wrap themselves in thermal ponchos.
Chat briefly on the prom donned in
neoprene hoods and wet suits before
one by one, diving in. Swim,
regardless of the weather,
goaded on by their coaches,
Jack Russell terriers, yapping
on the shore.

From now until May,
the flip-flop brigade are absent.
The beach belongs only to the dogs, and
those humans hardy enough to relish a
taste of the wild. United, they brace against
squalls and onshore winds, before
returning home for fresh bread and soup,
shared on sofas that have seen better days.
All reminiscing on how it feels
to be truly alive.
Their limbs and faces tingling,
the smell of salt still lingering in their hair.

FUDGE, THE READING COMPANION

Karen's face is red,
the same colour as her eyes and
her lips are sore and
that's no surprise coz
kids can be cruel,
mocking *why are you so slow to read?* and
deep within her body seethes at the taunt.

Mum cajoles to bring out the best in her
but, Nan doesn't help, *what's this dyslexia?*
Teachers are helpful, rarely bite, but there's always this pressure.
Their breath is creepy on the back of her head and
it's always worse when she's taking a test.
And there are SO many tests.

She sits in her room,
where unicorns gallop across the walls there are
rainbow curtains and glitter ball on the ceiling.
Karen is feeling, lonely. If only she had someone
undeniably reliable with no identifiable agenda
to befriend her.

Up jumps Fudge with a dangerous tail,
a nose for mischief
and eyes that never fail to say *if I could,
I would break down doors to be beside you.
One day I will die, and
break your heart but,
it will only make you love me more.*

Karen stares at a book.
Stops short of roaring her frustration,
enacting the temptation to
hurl it at the wall.
Instead she sprawls on the duvet,
starts reading out loud to her dog.

She recounts a tale of darkness and glory,
funny and scary, a feel-good story.
Where the heroine's chances are incredibly small
yet in a twist of fate, love conquers all.

The faithful Fudge just listens to her voice,
doesn't rise to the
stutter, splutter or the mutter of
mispronunciation.
Doesn't pass comment or try to correct,
doesn't expect anything.

Karen is free to practise her reading,
without force, or fuss, no if's, no but's
nothing alarming,
no need for Prince Charming;
just a little dog who is
helpful
without trying to help.
Comforting,
without trying to comfort.
Loving,
without trying to love.

Without ever knowing that
he is the hero,
saving the day, every day, and
worth his weight
in gold.

GROWN UP

Ilka is six.
She's a grown-up dog with
a puppy inside her, who
every now and then
tries to get out.

She's a brown snout, Girl Scout
on the look-out for mischief.
Assisted by a
lie low lurcher and
a street dog called Teddy.

Combat ready,
camouflaged by long grass they wait.
An eye-balling, stonewalling,
Mexican stand-off.
One twitch, and its game-on.
A rebel rumble, rough n'tumble,
mouth wrestling, second guessing
slapstick slalom.

Mind your backs!

Once the zoomies are done,
once every rabbit hole has been sniffed
and mole hill stripped of soil in a
dig and paw, claw frenzy of
find it if you can,
three friends on two legs stroll back
with three mates on four.

Indoors,
tongues lolling their contentment,
the dogs share chewy-chews, while
their humans, still
full of the thrill of watching,
dunk digestives in coffee
made with milk.

Later still,
once all are gone home,
the floor falling silent, the
puppy within Ilka sleeps,
while her grown-up self
creeps under the table,
pushes her head against the hand
that still bears the band of gold
from one taken too soon.

Ilka never met him,
yet she can still sense the loss.

FRIENDS FOREVER

On a floral chintz chair
in a dark, dusty hall,
sleeps Tessa, the cavalier,
curled in a ball.

Hidden from sight, the grand-father clock,
breaks the silence,
ticks and
tocks.

Other than that, the air is still
in the empty house at the top of the hill.

At the click of a key
Tess raises her head,
stiffly stretches,
gets out of bed.

Hello my pretty
croaks a familiar voice,
dropping her ears,
Tessa's tail rejoices
the return of her human,
bent over with age, with
sinewy hands like the bars of a cage.

They sit on a sofa draped with a throw,
the canine companion,
the ageing widow,
sharing a cake
sticky on top
bought in the High Street
from the bakers' shop.

Both of them smiling,
stalwarts together.
Scholars of life,
friends forever.

PEGGY THE COCKER-POO

Peggy,
a cocker-poo,
dog of many names,
terms of endearment,
love unashamed.

Peggy, becomes
Peggells,
when called in the park.
Or quite simply Peg! Exclamation mark.

She's The Pegster,
up to mischief.
Pegaloo,
her flamboyant self,
Or La Peg,
the biscuit thief,
known for cunning and stealth.

Then there's Pego,
Popoff, Pea-Pod, Peek-a-Boo,
Miss Peggy, Peggychops and
Peggo-poopie-doo.

She's a little dog of grandeur,
bit of megalomania,
digging her bed frantically,
Peg of Pegmania.

Murdering her toys,
simply Pegposterous.
Miss Poopichoop's smile
certainly isn't lost on us.

Her nicknames are endless.
Her memory auspicious.
And, when cuddled on the bed,
simply
Pegga-licous.

MABEL

Outdoors,
Mabel is labelled a tomboy. She is
the bottom poking from a bush
hunting for rabbits that were
never there. Her legs are
shorter than a cat, but
that's never been an issue.
Ignoring the whistle,
she runs,
lips pulled back, tongue flopping,
ears flapping, crashing through the brambles.
To infinity and beyond.

Indoors,
minus her sword and cape, this
mistress of mischief, runaway rebel,
rip snorting, rough, tough, digger, tigger of a terrier
is rendered helpless by the
tickle tummy touch of a hand,
cradled in the arms of
one who forgives and forgets, and
forgives and forgets again.
Deep down, this
jowly, growly gremlin genuinely wants to be good.
It isn't disobedience that leads her to stray.
It's just her ears have never quite mastered
the recall.

DON'T MAKE ME GO TO THE VETS

Don't make me go to the vets,
I'd rather stay at home,
let me hide under the blankets, safe in my comfort zone.
The waiting room, it frightens me,
all that barking and croaking.
And what about castrations?
Oh my God. You must be joking.

Then there's the needles, blood tests,
annual vaccinations,
the smell of surgical spirit from all those operations.
When I go through the door
I start to feel quite sick.
Remember the nurse and the clippers?
Bloody lunatic.

Last time, there was this Beagle,
he screamed when his nails were cut.
Plus a Chihuahua had a go at me,
sodding little mutt.

Don't make me go to the surgery.
Can't I stay at home with you?
We could walk to that café
for coffee and a choux.

*Oh, come my love,
you have to go,
it won't be so bad I'll bet.
And anyway,
we need the money,
and let's face it,
you are the vet.*

MEDICATION MAYHEM

A lady takes her dog to the vets,
the little dog's old, and occasionally wets
the floor. She reckons something is wrong,
her dog drinks a lot, and often the pong
when he poos is unpleasant. He has halitosis.
Vet takes a look, makes a diagnosis.
Just showing his age. No sign of dereliction.
It's renal disease, here, take this prescription.

Once home she takes a pill from the box.
Calls her dog, who sits on his hocks.
She tips back his head, to open his jaw,
the dog objects, starts to claw,
pushes her away. She drops the pill.
The little dog growls. If looks could kill.
Undeterred, she won't be defeated.
She has another go. Mission completed.

Well no, not quite. See, there's the pill on the carpet.
The dog spat it out. The little varmint.
She picks it up, but her fingers are sticky.
The pill starts to melt. This could be tricky.
She gets another, and wipes her hands clean.
But where's the dog? He's nowhere to be seen.
She calls him back, has another go.
Mission accomplished. Bingo.

No. See, when she opens his jaw,
she misses her aim, the pill hits the floor.
Then she nicks her thumb on a tush.
It starts to bleed. She heads off in a rush
to give it a wash. Grabs a plaster.
Steps on the pill. It crushes. Disaster.
She checks the packet. She's still got loads.
But, fails again. Her face explodes.

She phones the surgery. Speaks to a nurse,
colourful language, occasional curse.
Buys a solution, and calls to collect
a tweezery plunger, and this I'll bet
will save bloodied fingers. Put the pill in the tweezer,
insert in dog's mouth, use the plunger to lever
the pill down the throat. See, simple as that.
Success at last. Pat on the back.

That's what she thinks in this moment in time.
The dog toddles off, and everything's fine.
The tweezery plunger goes onto the shelf,
with the box of pills and everything else.
Then a small white thing catches her eye.
She bends down to see and, *Oh Jesus Chri…!*
The wretched tablet fell out of the end.
What to do next? Phone a friend?

She shakes her head, refills the plunger,
no one need know of this stupid blunder.
Goes up the garden in search of her hound,
grabs his throat, wrestles him to the ground.
Tweezers inserted, the plunger is pressed.
Blood pressure rising, she's ever so stressed.
But at last, it's done. The ordeal's over.
She pats the dog. *Good boy, Rover.*

What do you think? It's not as easy as that.
She looks at the tweezers. Oh no, what a prat.
The pill's still in there. It was never released.
No wonder the dog ran off looking pleased.
Now what she wonders. Her voice starts to quaver.
Can't do it alone. Best ask a neighbour.
Who suggests she puts the pill in a treat.
Blimey, how obvious. Wrap it in meat.

She waits till meal time, food is delicious.
Hides the pill. I know it's surreptitious
but needs must and all that, in the interests of health,
to get the job done, the best option is stealth.
Oh, this is simple, the dog even sits,
hairy tail thumping, chews up the bits.
Easy peasy, he's hoovered and gone.
The job is over. Or is it? Hang on…

Yes, you've guessed. You're one step ahead.
She clutches the bowl, her eyes misty red.
Although it's licked clean, one thing remains,
the pill is uneaten. That dog's got brains.
She eyes her dog. He eyeballs back.
If only the pill was a tasty snack.
Lightbulb moment. Her heart starts to flutter,
smear the pill with peanut butter.

It seems to have the desired effect.
The dog is fooled, he doesn't suspect
the peanutty goo wedged on her thumb,
conceals a tablet, 'til it hits his tongue.
Then, with the force of a ball from a cannon
he fires the pill. It bounces and lands on
the nose of the cat, who hisses and spits.
Oh, gimme a break! You, awkward little git.

The dog's affronted. He feels mistreated.
The box of pills is looking depleted.
She out of ideas so, it's back to the vets,
expert at dealing with wily old pets.
Use a syringe to fire a paste.
Easy to use and much less waste.
Your dog won't object if you're asking me.
That'll be sixty pounds fifty, plus VAT.

Back home she preps and arms the syringe.
Approaches her dog who starts to cringe.
She crouches down to his eye level,
Holds him tight. But the little devil
wriggles his arse as she touches his lips.
She starts to panic. The nozzle slips.
Like pus from a pimple, the paste lets fly,
catching her right, bang, in the eye.

She wipes her face, and continues to endeavour
to administer the dose, but her dog is really clever.
At the very last moment he swings his head,
splattering paste all over the bed.
Then, he clamps his jaws firmly shut.
Oh, open your gob! You, poxy little mutt!
He flings her a look. *Well, if you're gonna get rough.*
Flicks his tail and goes off in a huff.

He goes down the garden. Sits in the shed,
worries his toys, and digs up the bed.
*How dare she poke that thing in my face
without even asking. Bloody disgrace.*
She approaches, contrite. *Is she clutching a treat?
It's meaty and gooey, and so nice to eat*
he thinks, as it washes over his tongue.
She can't believe it. My God, she's just won!

He took the paste without a commotion,
because she pushed gently, in very slow motion.
OK, it may take several goes,
before the dog actually gets the right dose.
But finally, our heroine has got the technique.
So, the future is rosy, where once it was bleak.
The dog will stay healthy, his owner, his friend.

Mission accomplished.

Thank you

THE END